NINJA FOODI GRILL COOKBOOK FOR BEGINNERS

DILAN YUANG

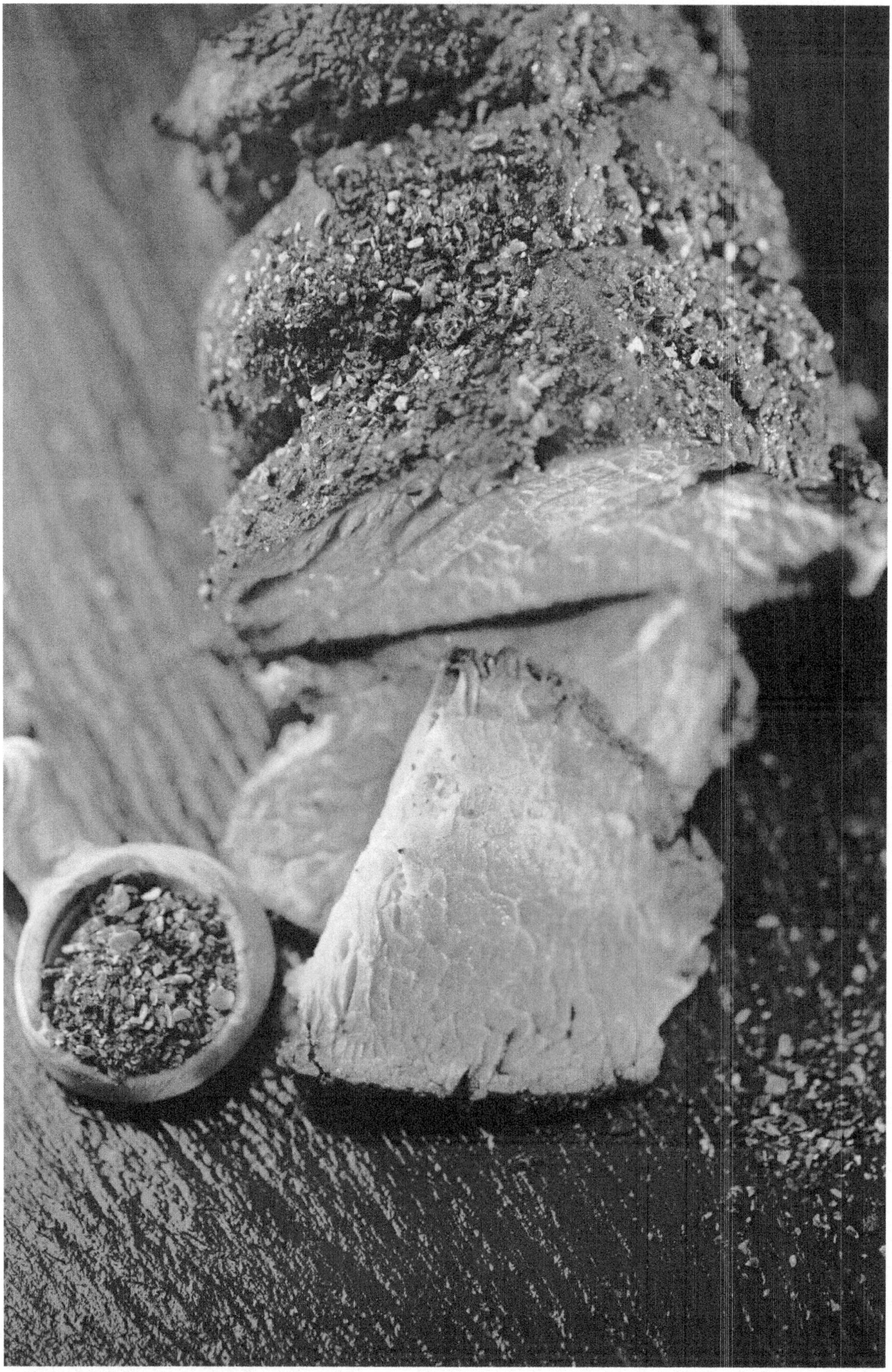

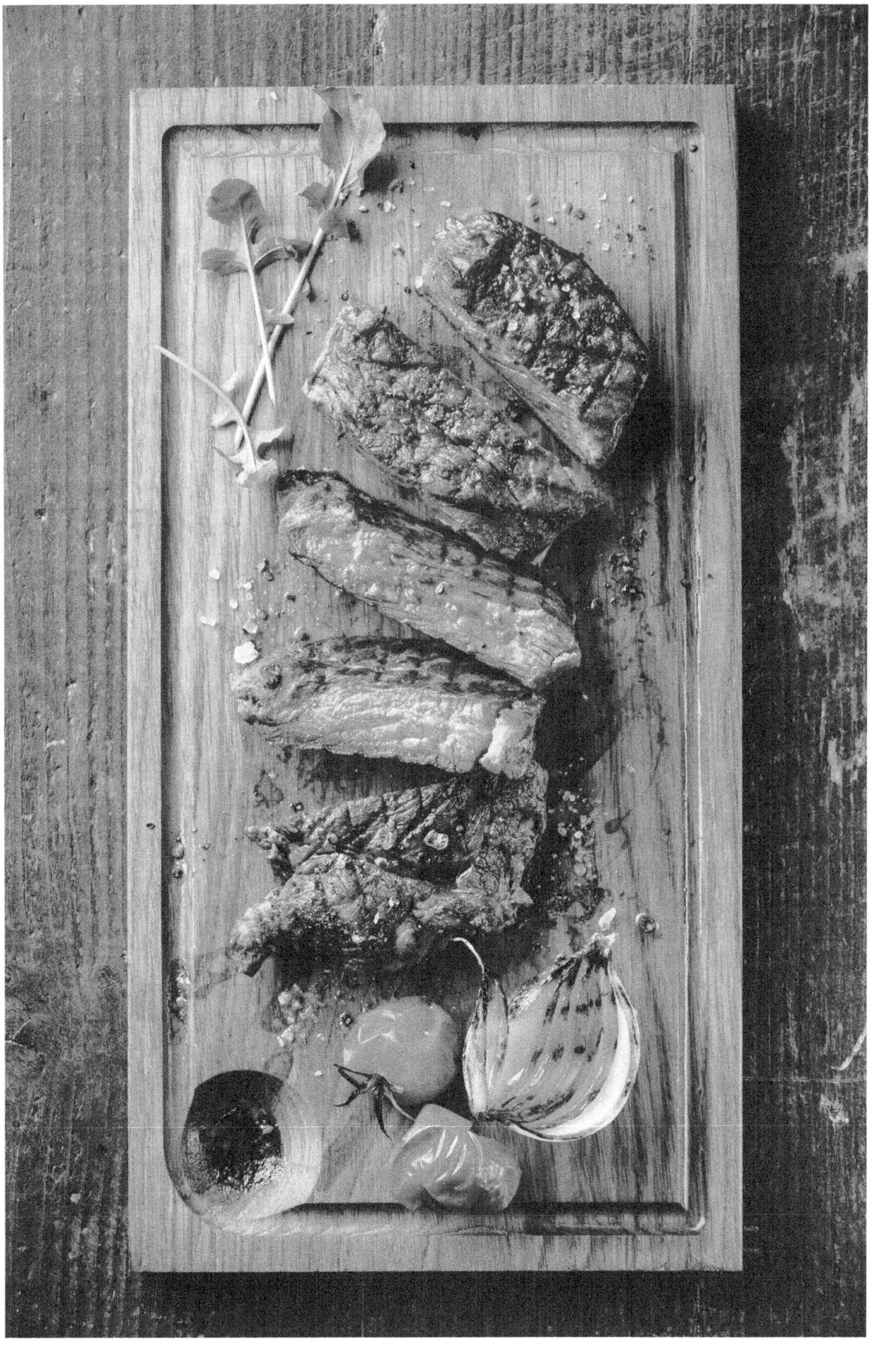

Copyright © 2020 by Dilan Yuang - All rights reserved.

This document is geared towards providing exact and reliable information in regards to the topic and issue covered. The publication is sold on the idea that the publisher is not required to render an accounting, officially permitted, or otherwise, qualified services. If advice is necessary, legal or professional, a practiced individual in the profession should be ordered.

From a Declaration of Principles which was accepted and approved equally by a Committee of the American Bar Association and a Committee of Publishers and Associations.

In no way is it legal to reproduce, duplicate, or transmit any part of this document by either electronic means or in printed format. Recording of this publication is strictly prohibited and any storage of this document is not allowed unless with written permission from the publisher. All rights reserved.

The information provided herein is stated to be truthful and consistent, in that any liability, regarding inattention or otherwise, by any usage or abuse of any policies, processes, or directions contained within is the solitary and utter responsibility of the recipient reader. Under no circumstances will any legal responsibility or blame be held against the publisher for any reparation, damages, or monetary loss due to the information herein, either directly or indirectly.

Respective authors own all copyrights not held by the publisher.

The information herein is offered for informational purposes solely and is universal as so. The presentation of the information is without a contract or any guarantee assurance.

The trademarks that are used are without any consent, and the publication of the trademark is without permission or backing by the trademark owner. All trademarks and brands within this book are for clarifying purposes only and are the owned by the owners themselves, not affiliated with this document.

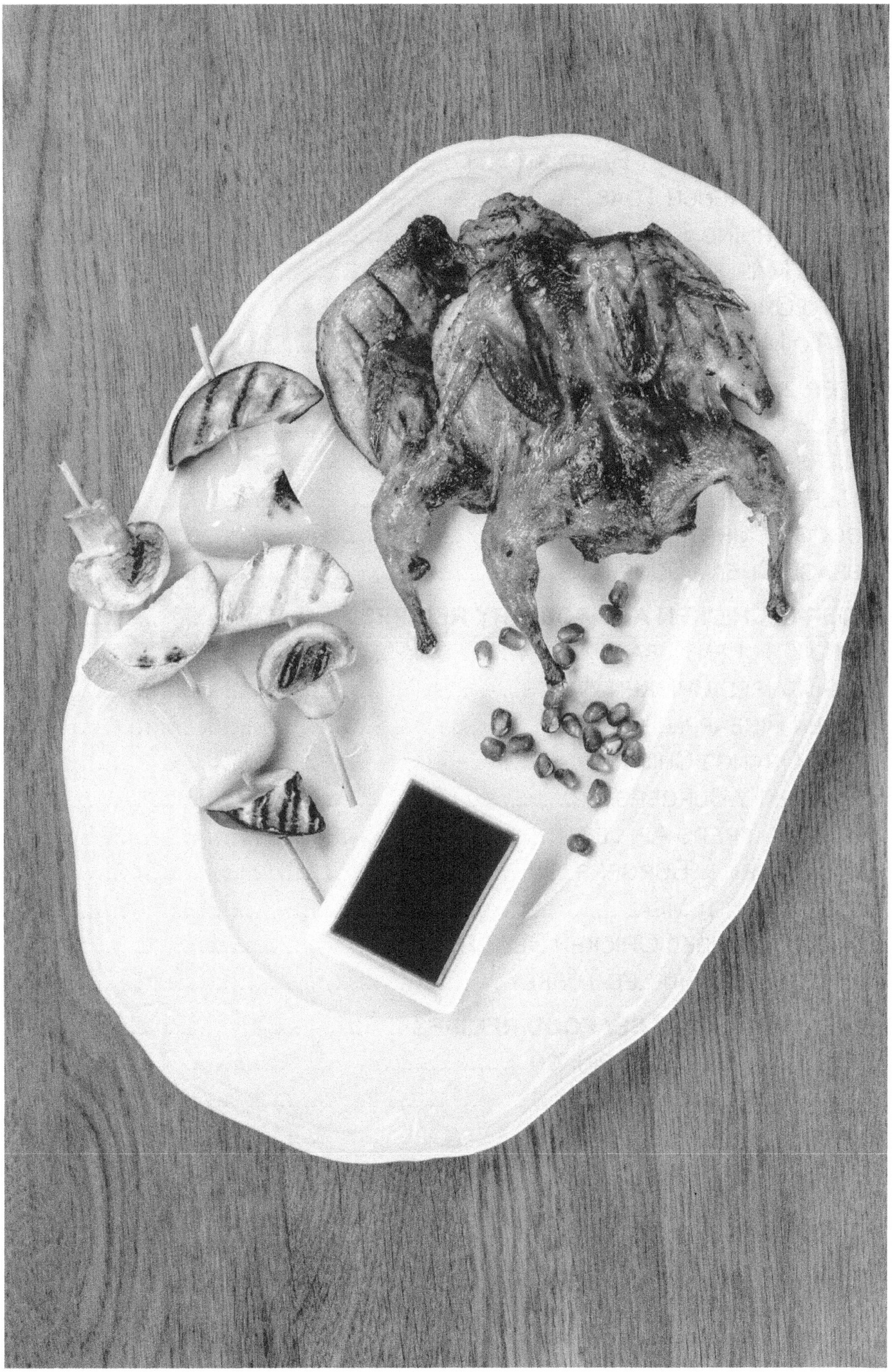

CONTENTS

CHAPTER 1: BREAKFAST 8
   Coconut Breakfast Bagels 8
   Pineapple French Toast 10
   Early Morning Sausage 12
   Grilled Maple Broccoli 13
   Potato Chips 14
   Easy To Make Beans 15

CHAPTER 2: VEGETARIAN AND VEGAN RECIPES 16
   Spinach Paneer Soup Meal 16
   Wholesome Veggie Delight 18
   Ginger Cauliflower Rice 20
   Broccoli Curry 22
   Cabbage Cream Soup 24

CHAPTER 3: CHICKEN AND POULTRY RECIPES 26
   Spiced Chicken Kebabs 26
   Beer-Braised Chicken Wings 28
   Chicken Pineapple Kebabs 30
   Garlic Orange Chicken 31
   Feta Turkey Burgers 33
   Chicken Alfredo Apples 35
   Classic Turkey Burgers 37
   Turkey Yogurt Meal 39
   Orange Flavored Chicken Delight 41
   Thanks Giving Grilled Turkey 42

CHAPTER 4: FISH AND SEAFOOD RECIPES 43
   Wholesome Salmon Spinach 43
   Tilapia & Green Cabbage 45
   Spinach Fish Curry 47
   Shrimp & Mayonnaise Rice 49
   Shrimp Tomato Dinner 51
   Spinach Cream Fish 53
   Salmon with Quinoa & Green Beans 55
   Fish Tomato & Olives 57

Awesome Mustard Cod 59
Grilled Fish With Caper Sauce 60

CHAPTER 5: BEEF AND PORK RECIPES 61
Tender Pineapple Flavored Steak 61
Red Wine Roasted Brisket 62
Herbed Lamb Chops 63
Herb Roasted Beef 64
Asian Style Apple Steak 66
Sherried Pork Roast 68
Coffee Flavored Steak 69
Easy Going Avocado And Beef Dish 70

CHAPTER 6: SNACKS 71
Cajuned Eggplant Appetizer 71
Honeyed Asparagus 72
Grilled Maple Broccoli 73
Potato Chips 74
Grilled Cheese Pineapple 75
Homely Honey Flavored Asparagus 77
Subtle Italian Squash 78

CHAPTER 7: DESSERT 79
Ranch Flavored Cauliflower Steak 79
Choco Pecan Fudge 81

Chapter 1: Breakfast

Coconut Breakfast Bagels

Prep Time: 5-10 min.

Cooking Time: 8 min.

Number of Servings: 4

Ingredients:

1 cup fine sugar

2 tablespoons black coffee, prepared and cooled down

4 bagels, halved

1/4 cup coconut milk

2 tablespoons coconut flakes

Directions:

1. Take Ninja Foodi Grill, arrange it over your kitchen platform, and open the top lid.
2. Arrange the grill grate and close the top lid.
3. Press "GRILL" and select the "MED" grill function. Adjust the timer to 4 minutes and then press "START/STOP." Ninja Foodi will start pre-heating.
4. Ninja Foodi is preheated and ready to cook when it starts to beep. After you hear a beep, open the top lid.
5. Arrange 2 bagels over the grill grate.
6. Close the top lid and cook for 2 minutes. Now open the top lid, flip the bagels.
7. Close the top lid and cook for 2 more minutes.
8. Allow cooking until the timer reads zero. Divide into serving plates.
9. Grill the remaining bagels in a similar way. In a mixing bowl, whisk the remaining ingredients.
10. Serve the grilled bagels with the prepared sauce on top.

Nutritional Values (Per Serving):

Calories: 395
Fat: 23g
Saturated Fat: 12g
Trans Fat: 0g
Carbohydrates: 42.5g

Fiber: 4g
Sodium: 358mg
Protein: 18.5g

Pineapple French Toast

Prep Time: 5-10 min.

Cooking Time: 15 min.

Number of Servings: 4-5

Ingredients:

10 bread slices

1/4 cup sugar

1/4 cup milk

3 large eggs

1 cup coconut milk

10 slices pineapple (1/4-inch-thick), peeled

1/2 cup coconut flakes

Cooking spray

Directions:

1. In a mixing bowl, whisk the coconut milk, sugar, eggs, and milk. Dip the bread in this mixture and set aside for about 2 minutes.
2. Take Ninja Foodi Grill, arrange it over your kitchen platform, and open the top lid.
3. Arrange the grill grate and close the top lid.
4. Press "GRILL" and select the "MED" grill function. Adjust the timer to 4 minutes and then press "START/STOP." Ninja Foodi will start pre-heating.
5. Ninja Foodi is preheated and ready to cook when it starts to beep. After you hear a beep, open the top lid.
6. Arrange half the bread slices over the grill grate.
7. Close the top lid and cook for 2 minutes. Now open the top lid, flip the slices.
8. Close the top lid and cook for 2 more minutes.
9. Allow cooking until the timer reads zero. Divide into serving plates.
10. Repeat with the remaining slices. And then grill the pineapple slices with the same amount of time (flipping after 2 minutes).
11. Serve warm with the grilled bread topped with some coconut flakes.

Nutritional Values (Per Serving):

Calories: 202
Fat: 15g
Saturated Fat: 4g

Trans Fat: 0g
Carbohydrates: 49g
Fiber: 3g
Sodium: 214mg
Protein: 8g

Early Morning Sausage

Prep Time: 10 minutes

Cooking Time: 10 minutes

Number of Servings: 4

Ingredients:

- 1 medium sweet yellow onion
- 4 medium eggs
- 4 sausage links
- 2 cups kale, chopped
- 1 cup mushrooms
- Olive oil as needed

Method:

1. Take your Ninja Foodi Grill and open lid, arrange grill grate and close top
2. Pre-heat Ninja Foodi by pressing the "GRILL" option and setting it to "HIGH" and timer to 5 minutes
3. let it pre-heat until you hear a beep
4. Arrange sausages over grill grate, lock lid and cook for 2 minutes, flip sausages and cook for 3 minutes more
5. Take sausages out
6. Take a baking pan and spread onion, kale, mushrooms, sausages and crack eggs on top
7. Arrange pan inside the grill and used the "BAKE" option to bake it at 350 degrees F for 5 minutes
8. Once done, open lid and serve
9. Enjoy!

Nutritional Values (Per Serving)

- Calories: 236
- Fat: 12 g
- Saturated Fat: 2 g
- Carbohydrates: 17 g
- Fiber: 4 g
- Sodium: 369 mg
- Protein: 18 g

Grilled Maple Broccoli

Prep Time: 5-10 min.

Cooking Time: 10 min.

Number of Servings: 4

Ingredients:

2 heads broccoli, cut into florets

4 tablespoons soy sauce

2 tablespoons canola oil

4 tablespoons balsamic vinegar

2 teaspoons maple syrup

Red pepper flakes and sesame seeds to garnish

Directions:

1. In a mixing bowl, add the soy sauce, balsamic vinegar, oil, and maple syrup. Whisk well and add the broccoli; toss well.
2. Take Ninja Foodi Grill, arrange it over your kitchen platform, and open the top lid.
3. Arrange the grill grate and close the top lid.
4. Press "GRILL" and select the "MAX" grill function. Adjust the timer to 10 minutes and then press "START/STOP." Ninja Foodi will start pre-heating.
5. Ninja Foodi is preheated and ready to cook when it starts to beep. After you hear a beep, open the top lid.
6. Arrange the broccoli over the grill grate.
7. Close the top lid and allow to cook until the timer reads zero.
8. Divide into serving plates.
9. Serve warm with red pepper flakes and sesame seeds on top.

Nutritional Values (Per Serving):

Calories: 141
Fat: 7g
Saturated Fat: 1g
Trans Fat: 0g
Carbohydrates: 14g
Fiber: 4g
Sodium: 853mg
Protein: 4.5g

Potato Chips

Prep Time: 5-10 min.

Cooking Time: 8-10 hours

Number of Servings: 2-3

Ingredients:

1 sweet potato, peeled and cut into slices

½ teaspoon sea salt

½ tablespoon avocado oil

Directions:

1. In a mixing bowl, toss the slice, and oil until evenly coated. Season with the salt to taste.
2. Take Ninja Foodi Grill, arrange it over your kitchen platform, and open the top lid.
3. Arrange the Crisping Basket inside the pot.
4. Press "DEHYDRATE" and adjust the temperature to 120°F. Adjust the timer to 8 hours and then press "START/STOP." Ninja Foodi will start pre-heating.
5. Ninja Foodi is preheated and ready to cook when it starts to beep. After you hear a beep, open the top lid.
6. Arrange the slices in a single layer directly inside the basket.
7. Close the top lid and allow it to cook until the timer reads zero. Dehydrate for 2 more hours if the slices are not crisp enough.
8. Serve warm.

Nutritional Values (Per Serving):

Calories: 146
Fat: 5g
Saturated Fat: 1g
Trans Fat: 0g
Carbohydrates: 22.5g
Fiber: 2g
Sodium: 651mg
Protein: 2g

Easy To Make Beans

Prep Time: 5 minutes

Cooking Time: 10 minutes

Number of Servings: 4

Ingredients:

- 1-pound green beans, trimmed
- 2 tablespoons vegetable oil
- 1 lemon, juiced
- Pinch of red pepper flakes
- Flaky sea salt as needed
- Fresh ground black pepper as needed

Method:

1. Take a medium-sized bowl and add green beans
2. Pre-heat Ninja Foodi by pressing the "GRILL" option and setting it to "MAX" and timer to 10 minutes
3. Let it pre-heat until you hear a beep
4. Once preheated, transfer green beans to Grill Grate
5. Lock lid and let them grill for 8-10 minutes, making sure to toss them from time to time until all sides are blustered well
6. Squeeze lemon juice over green beans and top with red pepper flakes, season with salt and pepper

Nutritional Values (Per Serving)

- Calories: 100
- Fat: 7 g
- Saturated Fat: 1 g
- Carbohydrates: 10 g
- Fiber: 4 g
- Sodium: 30 mg
- Protein: 2 g

Chapter 2: Vegetarian And Vegan Recipes

Spinach Paneer Soup Meal

Prep Time: 5-10 min.

Cooking Time: 5 min.

Number of Servings: 4

Ingredients:

1 tablespoon ginger, chopped

1 large yellow onion, chopped

2 teaspoons olive oil

5 garlic cloves, chopped

½ jalapeno chile, chopped

1 pound chopped spinach

2 tomatoes, chopped

2 teaspoons Garam masala

1 teaspoon ground turmeric

1 teaspoon salt

2 teaspoons ground cumin

½ teaspoon cayenne pepper

½ cup water

1 ½ cup paneer cubes (Indian cheese)

½ cup heavy whip cream

Directions:

1. Take Ninja Foodi multi-cooker, arrange it over a cooking platform, and open the top lid.

2. In the pot, add the oil; Select "SEAR/SAUTÉ" mode and select "MD: HI" pressure level. Press "STOP/START." After about 4-5 minutes, the oil will start simmering.
3. Add the ginger, garlic, chili, and cook (while stirring) until it becomes softened for 2-3 minutes.
4. Add the onions, spinach, tomatoes, turmeric, cumin, cayenne, garam masala, salt, and water. Stir the mixture.
5. Seal the multi-cooker by locking it with the pressure lid; ensure to keep the pressure release valve locked/sealed.
6. Select "PRESSURE" mode and select the "HI" pressure level. Then, set timer to 2 minutes and press "STOP/START"; it will start the cooking process by building up inside pressure.
7. When the timer goes off, naturally release inside pressure for about 8-10 minutes. Then, quick-release pressure by adjusting the pressure valve to the VENT. After pressure gets released, open the pressure lid.
8. Puree the mixture in a blender. Serve warm with some cream on top.

Nutritional Values (Per Serving):

Calories:

Fat: g

Saturated Fat: g

Trans Fat: 0g

Carbohydrates: g

Fiber: g

Sodium: mg

Protein: g

Wholesome Veggie Delight

Prep Time: 5 min.

Cooking Time: 10 min.

Number of Servings: 4

Ingredients:

½ cup kale leaves, chopped

1 tablespoon lemon juice

½ cup spinach, chopped

1 cups cauliflower, chopped

1 teaspoon mustard

½ teaspoon pepper

6 whole eggs

½ teaspoon salt

2 garlic cloves

3 teaspoons coconut oil

Directions:

1. Take Ninja Foodi multi-cooker, arrange it over a cooking platform, and open the top lid.
2. In the pot, add the oil; Select "SEAR/SAUTÉ" mode and select "MD: HI" pressure level. Press "STOP/START." After about 4-5 minutes, the oil will start simmering.
3. Add the garlic and cook (while stirring) until it becomes fragrant.
4. Add the cauliflower and stir-cook for 4-5 minutes. Add all the ingredients except eggs; stir-cook for 2 minutes. Stir in eggs.
5. Seal the multi-cooker by locking it with the pressure lid; ensure to keep the pressure release valve locked/sealed.
6. Select "PRESSURE" mode and select the "HI" pressure level. Then, set timer to 2 minutes and press "STOP/START"; it will start the cooking process by building up inside pressure.

7. When the timer goes off, quick release pressure by adjusting the pressure valve to the VENT. After pressure gets released, open the pressure lid. Serve warm.

Nutritional Values (Per Serving):

Calories: 475

Fat: 33.5g

Saturated Fat: 1.5g

Trans Fat: 0g

Carbohydrates: 7g

Fiber: 1.5g

Sodium: 656mg

Protein: 22g

Ginger Cauliflower Rice

Prep Time: 5-10 min.

Cooking Time: 16 min.

Number of Servings: 4

Ingredients:

1 garlic clove, minced

¼ teaspoon minced ginger

1 head cauliflower, cut into florets

2 tablespoons butter

¼ teaspoon red pepper flakes

1 ½ tablespoon sesame oil

Ground black pepper and salt to taste

1 egg

2 tablespoons soy sauce

2 scallions, sliced

Directions:

1. Blend the cauliflower florets in a blender to make rice like structure.
2. Take Ninja Foodi multi-cooker, arrange it over a cooking platform, and open the top lid.
3. In the pot, add the butter; Select "SEAR/SAUTÉ" mode and select "MD: HI" pressure level.
4. Press "STOP/START." After about 4-5 minutes, the butter will melt. Add the garlic, ginger, and red pepper flakes and cook (while stirring) until they become softened.
5. Add the cauliflower rice; stir-cook for 3-4 minutes. Add the egg and stir-cook until scrambles. Add the soy sauce. Season with salt and black pepper.
6. Seal the multi-cooker by locking it with the crisping lid; ensure to keep the pressure release valve locked/sealed.

7. Select the "AIR CRISP" mode and adjust the 350°F temperature level. Then, set timer to 10 minutes and press "STOP/START"; it will start the cooking process by building up inside pressure.
8. When the timer goes off, quick release pressure by adjusting the pressure valve to the VENT. After pressure gets released, open the crisping lid. Serve warm with the scallions on top.

Nutritional Values (Per Serving):

Calories: 153

Fat: 12.5g

Saturated Fat: 2g

Trans Fat: 0g

Carbohydrates: 5g

Fiber: 1.5g

Sodium: 214mg

Protein: 3g

Broccoli Curry

Prep Time: 5-10 min.

Cooking Time: 28 min.

Number of Servings: 4

Ingredients:

2 garlic cloves, minced

2 tablespoons extra-virgin olive oil

½ onion, diced

1 carrot, diced

1 stalk celery, sliced

1 teaspoon minced fresh ginger

¼ teaspoon red pepper flakes

2 cups chicken broth

Black pepper (ground) and salt to taste

1 (14-ounce) can full-fat coconut milk

2 tablespoons curry powder

3 cups broccoli

Cilantro, chopped and lime wedges, for garnish

Directions:

1. Take Ninja Foodi multi-cooker, arrange it over a cooking platform, and open the top lid. In the pot, add the oil; Select "SEAR/SAUTÉ" mode and select "MD: HI" pressure level. In a bowl. Combine the broccoli and the remaining 1 tablespoon of olive oil.
2. Press "STOP/START." After about 4-5 minutes, the oil will start simmering. Add the onions and cook (while stirring) for 2-3 minutes until they become softened and translucent.
3. Add the garlic, ginger, and red pepper flakes; stir-cook 2 to 3 minutes. Add the carrot and celery; stir cook for 3-4 minutes. Add the coconut milk and stir.

4. Add the curry powder and stir to combine well. Mix in the broth. Season with salt and pepper. Seal the multi-cooker by locking it with the pressure lid; ensure to keep the pressure release valve locked/sealed.
5. Select "PRESSURE" mode and select the "HI" pressure level. Then, set timer to 10 minutes and press "STOP/START"; it will start the cooking process by building up inside pressure.
6. When the timer goes off, quick release pressure by adjusting the pressure valve to the VENT. After pressure gets released, open the pressure lid. Arrange a reversible rack in the pot and place the broccoli over it.
7. Select "BROIL" mode and select the "HI" pressure level. Then, set timer to 8 minutes and press "STOP/START"; it will start the cooking process by building up inside pressure.
8. When the timer goes off, quick release pressure by adjusting the pressure valve to the VENT. After pressure gets released, open the pressure lid.
9. Add the broccoli in serving bowls and place the broth mixture on top. Serve warm with a sprinkle of cilantro and a wedge of lemon and enjoy!

Nutritional Values (Per Serving):

Calories: 362

Fat: 29.5g

Saturated Fat: 4g

Trans Fat: 0g

Carbohydrates: 12.5g

Fiber: 5g

Sodium: 458mg

Protein: 8.5g

Cabbage Cream Soup

Prep Time: 5-10 min.

Cooking Time: 17 min.

Number of Servings: 6

Ingredients:

3 garlic cloves, minced

2 tablespoons unsalted butter

1 onion, sliced

1 large head green cabbage, roughly chopped

Black pepper (ground) and salt to taste

1 cup heavy (whipping) cream

6 cups vegetable broth

Directions:

1. Take Ninja Foodi multi-cooker, arrange it over a cooking platform, and open the top lid. In the pot, add the butter; Select "SEAR/SAUTÉ" mode and select "MD: HI" pressure level.
2. Press "STOP/START." After about 4-5 minutes, the butter will melt.
3. Add the onions and cook (while stirring) until they become softened and translucent. Add the garlic and cook for 2-3 minutes.
4. Add the cabbage. Season with salt and black pepper, add the vegetable broth, and stir the mixture.
5. Seal the multi-cooker by locking it with the pressure lid; ensure to keep the pressure release valve locked/sealed.
6. Select "PRESSURE" mode and select the "HI" pressure level. Then, set timer to 10 minutes and press "STOP/START"; it will start the cooking process by building up inside pressure.
7. When the timer goes off, quick release pressure by adjusting the pressure valve to the VENT. After pressure gets released, open the pressure lid.
8. Add the heavy cream. Season with salt and pepper. Serve warm and enjoy!

Nutritional Values (Per Serving):

Calories: 304

Fat: 19.5g

Saturated Fat: 5g

Trans Fat: 0g

Carbohydrates: 15g

Fiber: 5.5g

Sodium: 526mg

Protein: 9g

Chapter 3: Chicken And Poultry Recipes

Spiced Chicken Kebabs

Prep Time: 5-10 min.

Cooking Time: 15 min.

Number of Servings: 4

Ingredients:

1 pound boneless, skinless chicken breasts, cut in 2-inch cubes

1 tablespoon chili powder

2 teaspoons paprika

1 tablespoon ground cumin

1 tablespoon garlic powder

¼ teaspoon sea salt

¼ teaspoon ground black pepper

2 tablespoons extra-virgin olive oil

2 red bell peppers, seeded and cut into 1-inch cubes

1 red onion, quartered

Juice of 1 lime

Directions:

1. In a mixing bowl, add the cumin, garlic powder, chili powder, paprika, salt, and black pepper. Combine the ingredients to mix well with each other.
2. Take a zip-lock bag, add the chicken, 1 tablespoon oil, and half of the spice mixture. Shake well and refrigerate for 1 hour to marinate.
3. Take another zip-lock bag, add the bell pepper, onion, remaining oil, and remaining spice mixture. Shake well and refrigerate for 1 hour to marinate.

4. Take the skewers, thread the chicken, peppers, and onions. Thread alternatively.
5. Take Ninja Foodi Grill, arrange it over your kitchen platform, and open the top lid. Arrange the grill grate and close the top lid.
6. Press "GRILL" and select the "HIGH" grill function. Adjust the timer to 10 minutes and then press "START/STOP." Ninja Foodi will start pre-heating.
7. Ninja Foodi is preheated and ready to cook when it starts to beep. After you hear a beep, open the top lid. Arrange the skewers over the grill grate.
8. Close the top lid and cook for 5 minutes. Now open the top lid, flip the skewers.
9. Close the top lid and cook for 5 more minutes. Cook until the food thermometer reaches 165°F. Grill for 3-4 more minutes if needed. Serve warm with some lime juice drizzled.

Nutritional Values (Per Serving):

Calories: 253
Fat: 12.5g
Saturated Fat: 1g
Trans Fat: 0g
Carbohydrates: 11.5g
Fiber: 2.5g
Sodium: 208mg
Protein: 24.5g

Beer-Braised Chicken Wings

Prep Time: 10-15 min.

Cooking Time: 40 min.

Number of Servings: 2

Ingredients:

1 tablespoon garlic powder

1/2 cup BBQ sauce

2 tablespoons canola oil

1/2 cup beer

1 pound chicken wings

Salt and ground black pepper to taste

Directions:

1. In a mixing bowl, add the chicken wings and other ingredients. Combine well.
2. Take Ninja Foodi Grill, arrange it over your kitchen platform, and open the top lid. Arrange the grill grate and close the top lid.
3. Press "GRILL" and select the "MED" grill function. Adjust the timer to 25 minutes and then press "START/STOP." Ninja Foodi will start preheating.
4. Ninja Foodi is preheated and ready to cook when it starts to beep. After you hear a beep, open the top lid.
5. Arrange the chicken wings over the grill grate. Reserve the marinade.
6. Close the top lid and cook for 13 minutes. Now open the top lid, flip the chicken. Close the top lid and cook for 12 more minutes.
7. Take out the grill plate and set aside the cooked chicken.
8. In the pot, add the marinade. Press "ROAST" and adjust the temperature to 350°F. Adjust the timer to 15 minutes and then press "START/STOP."
9. Close the top lid and allow it to cook until the timer reads zero. Serve the chicken wings with the hot sauce.

Nutritional Values (Per Serving):

Calories: 546
Fat: 27g
Saturated Fat: 8.5g
Trans Fat: 0g
Carbohydrates: 19g

Fiber: 3.5g
Sodium: 448mg
Protein: 57g

Chicken Pineapple Kebabs

Prep Time: 5-10 min.

Cooking Time: 14 min.

Number of Servings: 4

Ingredients:

1 cup teriyaki sauce

1 pound chicken breasts (boneless, skinless), cut into 2-inch cubes

2 green bell peppers, seeded and cut into 1-inch cubes

2 cups pineapple, cut into 1-inch cubes

Directions:

1. Take a zip-lock bag, add ½ cup teriyaki sauce and chicken. Shake well and refrigerate for 30 minutes to marinate.
2. Take Ninja Foodi Grill, arrange it over your kitchen platform, and open the top lid.
3. Arrange the grill grate and close the top lid.
4. Press "GRILL" and select the "MED" grill function. Adjust the timer to 14 minutes and then press "START/STOP." Ninja Foodi will start preheating.
5. Take the skewers, thread the chicken, pineapple, and peppers. Thread alternatively.
6. Ninja Foodi is preheated and ready to cook when it starts to beep. After you hear a beep, open the top lid.
7. Arrange the skewers over the grill grate — Reserve marinade.
8. Close the top lid and allow it to cook until the timer reads zero. Baste the skewers in between with the remaining teriyaki sauce. Cook until the food thermometer reaches 165°F for chicken.
9. Serve warm.

Nutritional Values (Per Serving):

Calories: 246
Fat: 4g
Saturated Fat: 0g
Trans Fat: 0g
Carbohydrates: 24.5g
Fiber: 3g
Sodium: 1743mg
Protein: 28g

Garlic Orange Chicken

Prep Time: 5-10 min.

Cooking Time: 22 min.

Number of Servings: 4

Ingredients:

4 chicken breasts, bones removed

4 tablespoons olive oil

4 cloves garlic, minced

4 ounces orange juice

1 tablespoon vinegar

2 teaspoon turmeric powder

2 teaspoons oregano

½ teaspoon chili powder

Directions:

1. In a mixing bowl, add the ingredients. Combine well.
2. Refrigerate for 2-3 hours to marinate.
3. Take Ninja Foodi Grill, arrange it over your kitchen platform, and open the top lid.
4. Arrange the grill grate and close the top lid.
5. Press "GRILL" and select the "MED" grill function. Adjust the timer to 22 minutes and then press "START/STOP." Ninja Foodi will start preheating.
6. Ninja Foodi is preheated and ready to cook when it starts to beep. After you hear a beep, open the top lid.
7. Arrange the chicken over the grill grate.
8. Close the top lid and cook for 11 minutes. Now open the top lid, flip the chicken.
9. Close the top lid and cook for 11 more minutes. Serve warm.

Nutritional Values (Per Serving):

Calories: 586
Fat: 37.5g
Saturated Fat: 9g
Trans Fat: 0g
Carbohydrates: 11.5g

Fiber: 2g
Sodium: 358mg
Protein: 59g

Feta Turkey Burgers

Prep Time: 10 min.

Cooking Time: 16 min.

Number of Servings: 8

Ingredients:

2 1/2 cups spinach, chopped

3 garlic cloves, minced

1 tablespoon avocado oil

2 shallots, chopped

2/3 cup feta cheese, crumbled

1/2 teaspoon salt

1/4 teaspoon pepper

3/4 teaspoon Greek seasoning

2 pounds turkey ground

8 hamburger buns, split

Directions:

1. Stir-cook all the shallots for 2 minutes in a saucepan with some oil until softened. Add the spinach and garlic; cook until wilts.
2. In a mixing bowl, add the spinach mixture. Add the seasoning, beef, and feta cheese. Combine the ingredients to mix well with each other. Prepare 8 patties from the mixture.
3. Take Ninja Foodi Grill, arrange it over your kitchen platform, and open the top lid. Arrange the grill grate and close the top lid.

4. Press "GRILL" and select the "MED" grill function. Adjust the timer to 16 minutes and then press "START/STOP." Ninja Foodi will start pre-heating.
5. Ninja Foodi is preheated and ready to cook when it starts to beep. After you hear a beep, open the top lid.
6. Arrange two patties over the grill grate.
7. Close the top lid and cook for 8 minutes. Now open the top lid, flip the patties.
8. Close the top lid and cook for 8 more minutes — grill remaining patties in the same manner.
9. Prepare the burgers with your choice of toppings and buns; enjoy!

Nutritional Values (Per Serving):

Calories: 328
Fat: 12.5g
Saturated Fat: 3g
Trans Fat: 0g
Carbohydrates: 31.5g
Fiber: 6g
Sodium: 464mg
Protein: 39.5g

Chicken Alfredo Apples

Prep Time: 5-10 min.

Cooking Time: 20 min.

Number of Servings: 4

Ingredients:

1 large apple, wedged

1 tablespoon lemon juice

4 chicken breasts, halved

4 teaspoons chicken seasoning

4 slices provolone cheese

1/4 cup blue cheese, crumbled

1/2 cup Alfredo sauce

Directions:

1. Season the chicken in a bowl with chicken seasoning. In another bowl, toss the apple with lemon juice.
2. Take Ninja Foodi Grill, arrange it over your kitchen platform, and open the top lid.
3. Arrange the grill grate and close the top lid.
4. Press "GRILL" and select the "MED" grill function. Adjust the timer to 16 minutes and then press "START/STOP." Ninja Foodi will start pre-heating.
5. Ninja Foodi is preheated and ready to cook when it starts to beep. After you hear a beep, open the top lid.
6. Arrange the chicken over the grill grate.
7. Close the top lid and cook for 8 minutes. Now open the top lid, flip the chicken.
8. Close the top lid and cook for 8 more minutes.
9. Then after, grill the apple in the same manner for 2 minutes per side.
10. Serve the chicken with the apple, blue cheese, and alfredo sauce.

Nutritional Values (Per Serving):

Calories: 247
Fat: 19g
Saturated Fat: 3g
Trans Fat: 0g
Carbohydrates: 29.5g

Fiber: 2g
Sodium: 853mg
Protein: 14.5g

Classic Turkey Burgers

Prep Time: 5-10 min.

Cooking Time: 12 min.

Number of Servings: 4

Ingredients:

1 jalapeño pepper, seeded, stemmed, and minced

3 tablespoons bread crumbs

1 pound turkey, ground

½ red onion, minced

½ teaspoon cayenne pepper

1 ½ teaspoons ground cumin

1 teaspoon paprika

½ teaspoon sea salt

½ teaspoon ground black pepper

4 burger buns

Optional to include - Lettuce, tomato, cheese, and ketchup and mustard

Directions:

1. In a large mixing bowl, add the ground turkey, red onion, jalapeño pepper, bread crumbs, cumin, paprika, cayenne pepper, salt, and black pepper. Combine the mixture well.
2. Prepare four patties from the mixture.
3. Take Ninja Foodi Grill, arrange it over your kitchen platform, and open the top lid.
4. Arrange the grill grate and close the top lid.
5. Press "GRILL" and select the "MED" grill function. Adjust the timer to 12 minutes and then press "START/STOP." Ninja Foodi will start pre-heating.
6. Ninja Foodi is preheated and ready to cook when it starts to beep. After you hear a beep, open the top lid.
7. Arrange the patties over the grill grate.
8. Close the top lid and allow it to cook until timer reads zero.

9. Arrange the buns and place the patties over them. Add your choice of toppings: lettuce, tomato, cheese, ketchup, and/ or mustard. Serve fresh.

Nutritional Values (Per Serving):

Calories: 301
Fat: 13.5g
Saturated Fat: 3g
Trans Fat: 0g
Carbohydrates: 28.5g
Fiber: 3g
Sodium: 561mg
Protein: 25.5g

Turkey Yogurt Meal

Prep Time: 5-10 min.

Cooking Time: 20 min.

Number of Servings: 4

Ingredients:

14 ounces yogurt

1 tablespoon ginger, grated

2 turkey breasts, skinless, boneless and cubed

1 yellow onion, chopped

1 teaspoon turmeric powder

2 teaspoons olive oil

Black pepper (ground) and salt to taste

Directions:

1. Take Ninja Foodi multi-cooker, arrange it over a cooking platform, and open the top lid.
2. In the pot, add the oil, Select "SEAR/SAUTÉ" mode and select "MD: HI" pressure level. Press "STOP/START." After about 4-5 minutes, the oil will start simmering.
3. Add the onions and cook (while stirring) until they become softened and translucent for 4 minutes.
4. Add the ginger and turmeric, stir-cook for 1 more minute. Add remaining ingredients, stir gently.
5. Seal the multi-cooker by locking it with the pressure lid, ensure to keep the pressure release valve locked/sealed.
6. Select "PRESSURE" mode and select the "HI" pressure level. Then after, set timer to 20 minutes and press "STOP/START," it will start the cooking process by building up inside pressure.
7. When the timer goes off, naturally release inside pressure for about 8-10 minutes. Then, quick-release pressure by adjusting the pressure valve to the VENT.
8. Serve warm.

Nutritional Values (Per Serving):

Calories: 176
Fat: 4.5g

Saturated Fat: 0g
Trans Fat: 0g
Carbohydrates: 7g
Fiber: 0g
Sodium: 854mg
Protein: 21g

Orange Flavored Chicken Delight

Prep Time: 5-10 minutes

Cooking Time: 15 minutes

Number of Servings: 4

Ingredients:

- 2 teaspoons ground coriander
- ½ teaspoon garlic salt
- ¼ teaspoon ground black pepper
- 12 chicken wings
- 1 tablespoon canola oil
- ¼ cup butter, melted
- 3 tablespoons honey
- ½ cup of orange juice
- 1/3 cup Sriracha chili sauce
- 2 tablespoons lime juice
- ¼ cup cilantro, chopped

Method:

1. Coat chicken with oil, season with spices and let it chill for 2 hours
2. Add listed ingredients and keep it on the side, cook for 3-4 minutes in a saucepan
3. Pre-heat Ninja Foodi by pressing the "GRILL" option and setting it to "MED" and timer to 10 minutes
4. Let it pre-heat until you hear a beep
5. Arrange chicken over grill grate, cook for 5 minutes
6. Flip and let it cook for 5 minutes more
7. Serve with sauce on top, enjoy!

Nutritional Values (Per Serving)

- Calories: 320
- Fat: 14 g
- Saturated Fat: 4 g
- Carbohydrates: 19 g
- Fiber: 1 g
- Sodium: 258 mg
- Protein: 25 g

Thanks Giving Grilled Turkey

Prep Time: 5-10 minutes

Cooking Time: 20 minutes

Number of Servings: 6

Ingredients:

- 8 pieces (6 ounces each) turkey cutlets
- 4 tablespoons sage leaves
- 8 ham slices
- Pepper and salt to taste
- 2 tablespoons butter, melted

Method:

1. Season turkey cutlets with pepper and salt, wrap them with bacon and brush with butter and add sage leaves on top
2. Take a baking pan and grease with butter
3. Pre-heat Ninja Foodi by pressing the "BAKE" option and setting it to "350-degree F" and timer to 20 minutes
4. Let it pre-heat until you hear a beep
5. Arrange cutlets in a baking pan and transfer to Grill, let it cook until the timer runs out
6. Serve and enjoy!

Nutritional Values (Per Serving)

- Calories: 450
- Fat: 20 g
- Saturated Fat: 4 g
- Carbohydrates: 2 g
- Fiber: 0.5 g
- Sodium: 656 mg
- Protein: 51 g

Chapter 4: Fish And Seafood Recipes

Wholesome Salmon Spinach

Prep Time: 5-10 min.

Cooking Time: 10 min.

Number of Servings: 4

Ingredients:

½ cup chicken stock

1 tablespoon olive oil or vegetable oil

2 cups baby spinach

2 salmon fillets, boneless and cut into cubes

A pinch of ground black pepper and salt

1 tablespoon parsley, chopped

Directions:

1. Take Ninja Foodi multi-cooker, arrange it over a cooking platform, and open the top lid.
2. In the pot, add the oil; Select "SEAR/SAUTÉ" mode and select "MD: HI" pressure level.
3. Press "STOP/START." After about 4-5 minutes, the oil will start simmering.
4. Add the salmon and cook (while stirring) to soften and sear for 1 minute on each side.
5. Add other ingredients except for the parsley; stir the mixture.
6. Seal the multi-cooker by locking it with the pressure lid; ensure to keep the pressure release valve locked/sealed.
7. Select "PRESSURE" mode and select the "HI" pressure level. Then, set timer to 10 minutes and press "STOP/START"; it will start the cooking process by building up inside pressure.
8. When the timer goes off, naturally release inside pressure for about 8-10 minutes. Then, quick-release pressure by adjusting the pressure valve to the VENT.
9. After pressure gets released, open the pressure lid.

10. Serve warm with some chopped parsley on top and enjoy!

Nutritional Values (Per Serving):

Calories: 203

Fat: 7g

Saturated Fat: 1g

Trans Fat: 0g

Carbohydrates: 6.5g

Fiber: 2g

Sodium: 312mg

Protein: 18g

Tilapia & Green Cabbage

Prep Time: 5-10 min.

Cooking Time: 25 min.

Number of Servings: 4

Ingredients:

1 cup green cabbage, shredded

½ teaspoon chili powder

2 tablespoons avocado oil or vegetable oil

4 tilapia fillets, boneless

2 tablespoons parsley, chopped

Ground black pepper and salt to the taste

Directions:

1. Take a baking pan; grease it with some cooking spray, vegetable oil, or butter. Add the fish and other ingredients. Combine well.
2. Take Ninja Foodi multi-cooker, arrange it over a cooking platform, and open the top lid.
3. In the pot, add water and place a reversible rack inside the pot. Place the - over the rack.
4. Seal the multi-cooker by locking it with the crisping lid; ensure to keep the pressure release valve locked/sealed.
5. Select "BAKE/ROAST" mode and adjust the 380°F temperature level. Then, set timer to 25 minutes and press "STOP/START"; it will start the cooking process by building up inside pressure.
6. When the timer goes off, quick release pressure by adjusting the pressure valve to the VENT. After pressure gets released, open the pressure lid.
7. Serve warm and enjoy!

Nutritional Values (Per Serving):

Calories: 143

Fat: 4g

Saturated Fat: 0.5g

Trans Fat: 0g

Carbohydrates: 7.5g

Fiber: 2g

Sodium: 234mg

Protein: 22g

Spinach Fish Curry

Prep Time: 5-10 min.

Cooking Time: 5 min.

Number of Servings: 4

Ingredients:

1 tablespoon Thai red curry paste

½ cup water

1 (14-ounce) can coconut milk

Vegetable oil to cook

1 small onion, sliced

1 medium zucchini, cut into thick rounds

1 pound frozen cod or grouper fillets

1 teaspoon lime juice (optional)

1 small seeded red bell pepper, cut into bite-size pieces

1 small (5-ounce) bag baby spinach

1 cup cherry tomatoes, halved

2 tablespoons chopped basil

¼ cup roasted salted cashews, coarsely chopped

Directions:

1. ake Ninja Foodi multi-cooker, arrange it over a cooking platform, and open the top lid.
2. In the pot, add the oil; Select "SEAR/SAUTÉ" mode and select "MD: HI" pressure level.
3. Press "STOP/START." After about 4-5 minutes, the oil will start simmering.
4. Add the curry paste and cook (while stirring) to mix with the oil. Add the coconut milk and stir.
5. Add the water, zucchini, onion, bell pepper, and fish fillets; stir the mixture.

6. Seal the multi-cooker by locking it with the pressure lid; ensure to keep the pressure release valve locked/sealed.
7. Select "PRESSURE" mode and select the "LO" pressure level. Then, set timer to 3 minutes and press "STOP/START"; it will start the cooking process by building up inside pressure.
8. When the timer goes off, quick release pressure by adjusting the pressure valve to the VENT. After pressure gets released, open the pressure lid.
9. Make small pieces from the cooked fish.
10. Select "SEAR/SAUTÉ" mode and select the "MD" pressure level; add the tomatoes, lime juice, and spinach; combine. Stir-cook until heated through.
11. Serve warm with basil and cashews on top, and enjoy!

Nutritional Values (Per Serving):

Calories: 386

Fat: 24.5g

Saturated Fat: 16g

Trans Fat: 0g

Carbohydrates: 17g

Fiber: 4g

Sodium: 187mg

Protein: 25g

Shrimp & Mayonnaise Rice

Prep Time: 5-10 min.

Cooking Time: 10 min.

Number of Servings: 4

Ingredients:

16 ounces shrimps

½ cup mayonnaise

1 cup long-grain white rice

1 cup water

½ teaspoon Sriracha

¼ cup sweet chili sauce

2 tablespoons sliced scallions

Directions:

1. Take Ninja Foodi multi-cooker, arrange it over a cooking platform, and open the top lid.
2. In the pot, add the rice and water.
3. Seal the multi-cooker by locking it with the pressure lid; ensure to keep the pressure release valve locked/sealed.
4. Select "PRESSURE" mode and select the "HI" pressure level. Then, set timer to 2 minutes and press "STOP/START"; it will start the cooking process by building up inside pressure.
5. When the timer goes off, quick release pressure by adjusting the pressure valve to the VENT. After pressure gets released, open the pressure lid.
6. Over the rice, place the reversible rack; arrange the shrimps over.
7. Seal the multi-cooker by locking it with the crisping lid; ensure to keep the pressure release valve locked/sealed.
8. Select the "AIR CRISP" mode and adjust the 390°F temperature level. Then, set timer to 10 minutes and press "STOP/START"; it will start the cooking process by building up inside pressure.

9. When the timer goes off, quick release pressure by adjusting the pressure valve to the VENT.
10. After pressure gets released, open the pressure lid.
11. Take a mixing bowl, add the mayonnaise, sweet chili sauce, and Sriracha; combine well.
12. Add the shrimps and combine them well. Serve the shrimps with cooked rice and scallions on top.

Nutritional Values (Per Serving):

Calories: 413

Fat: 11g

Saturated Fat: 2g

Trans Fat: 0g

Carbohydrates: 46.5g

Fiber: 2g

Sodium: 628mg

Protein: 26g

Shrimp Tomato Dinner

Prep Time: 5-10 min.

Cooking Time: 2 min.

Number of Servings: 2

Ingredients:

½ teaspoon red pepper flakes

3 tablespoons unsalted butter

1 ½ cup onion, chopped

1 tablespoon garlic

1 can (14 ½ ounces) tomatoes, diced

1 pound shrimp, peeled

1 cup crumbled feta cheese

1 teaspoon dried oregano

1 teaspoon salt

½ cup parsley, chopped

½ cup black olives, sliced

Directions:

1. Take Ninja Foodi multi-cooker, arrange it over a cooking platform, and open the top lid.
2. In the pot, add the butter; Select "SEAR/SAUTÉ" mode and select "MD: HI" pressure level.
3. Press "STOP/START." After about 4-5 minutes, the butter will melt. Add the garlic, pepper flakes, and cook (while stirring) for 1 minute.
4. Add the onion, tomato, oregano, salt, and stir well. Add the shrimp and stir again.
5. Seal the multi-cooker by locking it with the pressure lid; ensure to keep the pressure release valve locked/sealed.
6. Select "PRESSURE" mode and select the "HI" pressure level. Then, set timer to 1 minute and press "STOP/START"; it will start the cooking process by building up inside pressure.

7. When the timer goes off, quick release pressure by adjusting the pressure valve to the VENT. After pressure gets released, open the pressure lid. Serve warm with the olives, feta, and parsley on top.

Nutritional Values (Per Serving):

Calories: 358

Fat: 21g

Saturated Fat: 2g

Trans Fat: 0g

Carbohydrates: 9.5g

Fiber: 2g

Sodium: 542mg

Protein: 29g

Spinach Cream Fish

Prep Time: 5-10 min.

Cooking Time: 5 min.

Number of Servings: 4

Ingredients:

Sauce:

14 ounces unsweetened coconut milk

1 tablespoon ginger root, minced

1 cup tomatoes, chopped

1 cup yellow onion, chopped

1 teaspoon garam masala powder

1 teaspoon ground turmeric

1 teaspoon cayenne pepper

1 tablespoon garlic, minced

2 cups chopped spinach

Salt to taste

¼ cup water

Fish:

1 pound semi-frozen haddock fillets, cut into 3-inch pieces

½ teaspoon ground turmeric

Salt to taste

2 tablespoons olive oil

Directions:

1. In a blender or food processor, add the tomatoes onion, ginger, garlic and ½ cup of coconut milk. Blend the mixture until it becomes smooth.

2. Coat the fish cubes with the oil; rub with the turmeric and salt to coat evenly. Add over a foil paper and seal the edges to make a pack.
3. Take Ninja Foodi multi-cooker, arrange it over a cooking platform, and open the top lid.
4. In the pot, add water, sauce, spinach, spices, salt, stir the mixture. Place a reversible rack inside the pot. Place the foil packet over the rack.
5. Seal the multi-cooker by locking it with the pressure lid; ensure to keep the pressure release valve locked/sealed.
6. Select "PRESSURE" mode and select the "HI" pressure level. Then, set timer to 5 minutes and press "STOP/START"; it will start the cooking process by building up inside pressure.
7. When the timer goes off, quick release pressure by adjusting the pressure valve to the VENT. After pressure gets released, open the pressure lid. Mix in the remaining coconut milk in the spinach sauce.
8. Add the fish in a serving plate; add the spinach sauce on top. Serve warm.

Nutritional Values (Per Serving):

Calories: 324

Fat: 21.5g

Saturated Fat: 4g

Trans Fat: 0g

Carbohydrates: 7.5g

Fiber: 2g

Sodium: 274mg

Protein: 20g

Salmon with Quinoa & Green Beans

Prep Time: 10 min.

Cooking Time: 10 min.

Number of Servings: 4

Ingredients:

4 (4-ounce) skinless salmon fillets

8 ounces green beans

1 cup quinoa, rinsed

1 ½ cups water

1 tablespoon extra-virgin olive oil

1 teaspoon sea salt

1 teaspoon black pepper, freshly ground

½ tablespoon brown sugar

½ tablespoon lemon juice

4 tablespoons (½ stick) unsalted butter, melted

2 garlic cloves, minced

½ teaspoon dried thyme

½ teaspoon dried rosemary

Directions:

1. Take Ninja Foodi multi-cooker, arrange it over a cooking platform, and open the top lid.
2. In the pot, add water, quinoa, and place a reversible rack inside the pot. Place the salmon fillets over the rack.
3. Seal the multi-cooker by locking it with the pressure lid; ensure to keep the pressure release valve locked/sealed.
4. Select "PRESSURE" mode and select the "HI" pressure level. Then, set timer to 2 minutes and press "STOP/START"; it will start the cooking process by building up inside pressure.

5. When the timer goes off, quick release pressure by adjusting the pressure valve to the VENT. After pressure gets released, open the pressure lid.
6. Take out the salmon fillet and reserve the cooked quinoa.
7. In a mixing bowl, toss the green beans with the olive oil, ½ teaspoon black pepper, and ½ teaspoon salt.
8. In a mixing bowl, combine the butter, brown sugar, lemon juice, garlic, thyme, rosemary, and remaining ½ teaspoon salt and black pepper. Add the salmon fillets and coat well.
9. In the pot, add the salmon mixture and top with the bean mixture.
10. Seal the multi-cooker by locking it with the crisping lid; ensure to keep the pressure release valve locked/sealed.
11. Select "BROIL" mode and select the "HI" pressure level. Then, set timer to 7 minutes and press "STOP/START"; it will start the cooking process by building up inside pressure.
12. When the timer goes off, quick release pressure by adjusting the pressure valve to the VENT.
13. After pressure gets released, open the pressure lid.
14. Serve warm with cooked quinoa and enjoy!

Nutritional Values (Per Serving):

Calories: 468

Fat: 22.5g

Saturated Fat: 8g

Trans Fat: 0g

Carbohydrates: 31.5g

Fiber: 6g

Sodium: 591mg

Protein: 29g

Fish Tomato & Olives

Prep Time: 5-10 min.

Cooking Time: 8 min.

Number of Servings: 4

Ingredients:

3 tablespoons olive oil

½ small onion, sliced (about ½ cup)

2 large garlic cloves, minced

4 (6-ounce) tilapia fillets

¼ teaspoon kosher salt

1 small jalapeño pepper, seeded and minced

1 bay leaf

1 (14.5-ounce) can diced tomatoes, drained

⅓ cup green olives, sliced

¼ cup chopped fresh parsley

½ teaspoon dried oregano leaves

3 tablespoons capers

Directions:

1. Sprinkle the fish with the salt.
2. Take Ninja Foodi multi-cooker, arrange it over a cooking platform, and open the top lid.
3. In the pot, add the oil; Select "SEAR/SAUTÉ" mode and select "MD: HI" pressure level.
4. Press "STOP/START." After about 4-5 minutes, the oil will start simmering.
5. Add the onions, jalapeno, garlic, and cook (while stirring) for 4-5 minutes until they become softened and translucent.
6. Add the tomatoes, bay leaf, oregano, olives, half the parsley, and half the capers; stir the mixture. Place the fish over.

7. Seal the multi-cooker by locking it with the pressure lid; ensure to keep the pressure release valve locked/sealed.
8. Select "PRESSURE" mode and select the "LO" pressure level. Then, set timer to 3 minutes and press "STOP/START"; it will start the cooking process by building up inside pressure.
9. When the timer goes off, quick release pressure by adjusting the pressure valve to the VENT. After pressure gets released, open the pressure lid.
10. Serve warm with remaining capers and parsley on top and enjoy!

Nutritional Values (Per Serving):

Calories: 326

Fat: 15g

Saturated Fat: 3g

Trans Fat: 0g

Carbohydrates: 8g

Fiber: 3g

Sodium: 591mg

Protein: 34.5g

Awesome Mustard Cod

Prep Time: 5-10 minutes

Cooking Time: 10 minutes

Number of Servings: 3

Ingredients:

- 1 large whole egg
- 1 teaspoon Dijon mustard
- ½ cup bread crumbs
- 1-pound cod filets
- ¼ cup all-purpose flour
- 1 tablespoon dried parsley
- 1 teaspoon paprika
- ½ teaspoon pepper

Method:

1. Take fish fillets and slice them into 1 inch wide strips
2. Take a mixing bowl and whisk in eggs, add mustard and combine well
3. Add flour in another bowl
4. Take another bowl and add bread crumbs, dried parsley, paprika, black pepper and combine well
5. Coat strips with flour, then coat with egg mix, coat with crumbs at last
6. Pre-heat Ninja Foodi by pressing the "AIR CRISP" option and setting it to "390 Degrees F" and timer to 10 minutes
7. Let it pre-heat until you hear a beep
8. Arrange strips directly inside basket, lock lid and cook until the timer runs out
9. Serve and enjoy!

Nutritional Values (Per Serving)

- Calories: 200
- Fat: 4 g
- Saturated Fat: 1 g
- Carbohydrates: 17 g
- Fiber: 1 g
- Sodium: 214 mg
- Protein: 24 g

Grilled Fish With Caper Sauce

Prep Time: 10 minutes

Cooking Time: 8 minutes

Number of Servings: 4

Ingredients:

- 4 swordfish steaks, about 1-inch thick
- 4 tablespoons unsalted butter
- 1 lemon, sliced into 8 slices
- 1 tablespoon lemon juice
- 1 tablespoon extra-virgin olive oil
- 2 tablespoons capers, drained
- Sea salt
- Black pepper, freshly grounded

Method:

1. Take a large shallow bowl and whisk together the lemon juice and oil
2. Season with swordfish steaks with salt and pepper on each side, place in the oil mixture
3. Turn to coat both sides and refrigerate for 15 minutes
4. Insert the grill grate and close the hood
5. Pre-heat Ninja Foodi by pressing the "GRILL" option at and setting it to "MAX" and timer to 8 minutes
6. Let it pre-heat until you hear a beep
7. Arrange the swordfish over the grill grate, lock lid and cook for 9 minutes
8. Place a medium saucepan over medium heat and melt butter
9. Add the lemon slices and capers to the pan and cook for 1 minute
10. Then turn off the heat
11. Remove the swordfish from the grill and serve with caper sauce over it
12. Enjoy!

Nutritional Values (Per Serving)

- Calories: 472
- Fat: 31 g
- Saturated Fat: 6 g
- Carbohydrates: 2 g
- Fiber: 0.5 g
- Sodium: 540 mg
- Protein: 48 g

Chapter 5: Beef And Pork Recipes

Tender Pineapple Flavored Steak

Prep Time: 5-10 minutes

Cooking Time: 8 minutes

Number of Servings: 4

Ingredients:

- ½ medium pineapple, cored and diced
- 1 jalapeno, seeded and stemmed, diced
- 1 medium red onion, diced
- 4 pieces filet mignon steaks, 6-8 ounces each
- 1 tablespoon canola oil
- Salt and pepper to taste
- 1 tablespoon lime juice
- ¼ cup cilantro leaves, chopped
- Chili powder and ground coriander

Method:

1. Rub fillets with oil evenly, season them well with salt and pepper
2. Pre-heat Ninja Foodi by pressing the "GRILL" option and setting it to "HIGH" and timer to 8 minutes
3. Let it pre-heat until you hear a beep
4. Arrange fillets over grill grate, lock lid and cook for 4 minutes until the internal temperature reaches 125 degrees F
5. Take a mixing bowl and add pineapple, onion, jalapeno, mix well
6. Add lime juice, cilantro, chili powder, coriander and combine
7. Serve fillets with the pineapple mixture on top
8. Enjoy!

<u>Nutritional Values (Per Serving)</u>

- Calories: 530
- Fat: 22 g
- Saturated Fat: 7 g
- Carbohydrates: 21 g
- Fiber: 4 g
- Sodium: 286 mg
- Protein: 58 g

Red Wine Roasted Brisket

Prep Time: 5-10 min.

Cooking Time: 45 min.

Number of Servings: 4

Ingredients:

3/4 cup red wine vinegar

1 large onion, sliced thinly

10 garlic cloves, minced

1 bunch cilantro, chopped

3-pounds beef brisket

Directions:

1. Take food processor or blender, open the lid and inside add the garlic, cilantro, red wine, and onions.
2. Blend to make a smooth mixture.
3. Take a zip-lock bag, add the garlic mixture, salt, pepper, and brisket in it. Shake well and refrigerate for 2-4 hours to marinate.
4. Take Ninja Foodi Grill, arrange it over your kitchen platform, and open the top lid. Lightly grease cooking pot with some oil or cooking spray.
5. Press "ROAST" and adjust the temperature to 350°F. Adjust the timer to 45 minutes and then press "START/STOP." Ninja Foodi will start pre-heating.
6. Ninja Foodi is preheated and ready to cook when it starts to beep. After you hear a beep, open the top lid.
7. Arrange the brisket directly inside the pot.
8. Close the top lid and allow it to cook until the timer reads zero.
9. Serve warm.

Nutritional Values (Per Serving):

Calories: 462
Fat: 16g
Saturated Fat: 5g
Trans Fat: 0g
Carbohydrates: 6.5g
Fiber: 1g
Sodium: 238mg
Protein: 56g

Herbed Lamb Chops

Prep Time: 5-10 min.

Cooking Time: 15 min.

Number of Servings: 2

Ingredients:

1 tablespoon rosemary, chopped

3 tablespoons extra-virgin olive oil

1 garlic clove, minced

½ rack lamb (4 bones)

Ground black pepper and salt to taste

Directions:

1. In a mixing bowl, add the oil, garlic, and rosemary. Combine the ingredients to mix well with each other.
2. Add the lamb, salt and pepper; coat well. Refrigerate for 2-4 hours to marinate.
3. Take Ninja Foodi Grill, arrange it over your kitchen platform, and open the top lid.
4. Arrange the grill grate and close the top lid.
5. Press "GRILL" and select the "HIGH" grill function. Adjust the timer to 12 minutes and then press "START/STOP." Ninja Foodi will start pre-heating.
6. Ninja Foodi is preheated and ready to cook when it starts to beep. After you hear a beep, open the top lid.
7. Arrange the lamb rack over the grill grate.
8. Close the top lid and cook for 6 minutes. Now open the top lid, flip the lamb.
9. Close the top lid and cook for 6 more minutes. Cook until the food thermometer reaches 145°F.
10. Serve warm.

Nutritional Values (Per Serving):

Calories: 362
Fat: 29.5g
Saturated Fat: 6.5g
Trans Fat: 0g
Carbohydrates: 2g
Fiber: 0.5g
Sodium: 328mg
Protein: 22g

Herb Roasted Beef

Prep Time: 5-10 min.

Cooking Time: 30 min.

Number of Servings: 4-6

Ingredients:

1 teaspoon basil

½ teaspoon thyme

2-pounds beef round roast

1 onion, sliced thinly

3 tablespoons olive oil

½ cup water

¼ teaspoon black pepper

1 teaspoon salt

Directions:

1. In a mixing bowl, add all the ingredients. Combine the ingredients to mix well with each other.
2. Add the roast and coat well. Set aside for 15-30 minutes.
3. Take Ninja Foodi Grill, arrange it over your kitchen platform, and open the top lid. Lightly grease cooking pot with some oil or cooking spray.
4. Press "ROAST" and adjust the temperature to 380°F. Adjust the timer to 20 minutes and then press "START/STOP." Ninja Foodi will start pre-heating.
5. Ninja Foodi is preheated and ready to cook when it starts to beep. After you hear a beep, open the top lid.
6. Arrange the roast directly inside the pot.
7. Close the top lid and cook for 10 minutes. Now open the top lid, flip the roast.
8. Close the top lid and cook for 10 more minutes.
9. Carve the roast and serve warm.

Nutritional Values (Per Serving):

Calories: 326
Fat: 13g
Saturated Fat: 3g
Trans Fat: 0g

Carbohydrates: 7g
Fiber: 1g
Sodium: 502mg
Protein: 46g

Asian Style Apple Steak

Prep Time: 5-10 min.

Cooking Time: 13 min.

Number of Servings: 4

Ingredients:

3 tablespoons sesame oil

3 tablespoons brown sugar

1 ½ pounds beef tips

4 garlic cloves, minced

½ apple, peeled and grated

⅓ cup soy sauce

1 teaspoon ground black pepper

Sea salt to taste

Directions:

1. In a mixing bowl, add the garlic, apple, sesame oil, sugar, soy sauce, pepper, and salt. Combine the ingredients to mix well with each other.
2. Add the beef and coat well. Refrigerate for 1-2 hours to marinate.
3. Take Ninja Foodi Grill, arrange it over your kitchen platform, and open the top lid.
4. Arrange the grill grate and close the top lid.
5. Press "GRILL" and select the "MED" grill function. Adjust the timer to 14 minutes and then press "START/STOP." Ninja Foodi will start pre-heating.
6. Ninja Foodi is preheated and ready to cook when it starts to beep. After you hear a beep, open the top lid.
7. Arrange the beef over the grill grate.
8. Close the top lid and allow to cook until the timer reads 11 minutes. Cook until the food thermometer reaches 145°F. If needed, cook for 3 more minutes.
9. Slice and serve warm.

Nutritional Values (Per Serving):

Calories: 517
Fat: 29g
Saturated Fat: 10.5g
Trans Fat: 0g
Carbohydrates: 16.5g

Fiber: 2g
Sodium: 1198mg
Protein: 36g

Sherried Pork Roast

Prep Time: 5-10 min.

Cooking Time: 45-50 min.

Number of Servings: 4

Ingredients:

1/4 cup dry sherry

3 tablespoons honey

2-pounds pork roast, trimmed

1/3 cup soy sauce

2 cloves of garlic, minced

½ teaspoon ground ginger

Directions:

1. In a mixing bowl, add all the ingredients. Combine the ingredients to mix well with each other.
2. Add the pork roast and combine it well. Refrigerate for 10-12 hours to marinate.
3. Take Ninja Foodi Grill, arrange it over your kitchen platform, and open the top lid. Lightly grease cooking pot with some oil or cooking spray.
4. Press "ROAST" and adjust the temperature to 400°F. Adjust the timer to 25 minutes and then press "START/STOP." Ninja Foodi will start pre-heating.
5. Ninja Foodi is preheated and ready to cook when it starts to beep. After you hear a beep, open the top lid.
6. Arrange the roast directly inside the pot.
7. Close the top lid and cook for 15 minutes. Now open the top lid, flip the roast.
8. Close the top lid and cook for 10 more minutes.
9. Serve warm.

Nutritional Values (Per Serving):

Calories: 524
Fat: 19g
Saturated Fat: 6g
Trans Fat: 0g
Carbohydrates: 20.5g
Fiber: 2g
Sodium: 851mg
Protein: 58g

Coffee Flavored Steak

Prep Time: 10 minutes

Cooking Time: 50 minutes

Number of Servings: 4

Ingredients:

- 1 and ½ pounds beef flank steak
- 1 teaspoon instant espresso powder
- ½ teaspoon garlic powder
- 2 teaspoons chili powder
- 2 tablespoons olive oil
- Salt and pepper, to taste

Method:

1. Insert the grill grate and close the hood
2. Pre-heat Ninja Foodi by pressing the "GRILL" option at and setting it to "HIGH" and timer to 40 minutes
3. Once it pre-heat until you hear a beep
4. Make the dry rub by mixing the chili powder, espresso powder, garlic powder, salt, and pepper
5. Rub all over the steak and brush with oil
6. Place on the grill grate and cook for 40 minutes
7. Flip after 20 minutes
8. Serve and enjoy!

Nutritional Values (Per Serving)

- Calories: 250
- Fat: 14 g
- Saturated Fat: 4 g
- Carbohydrates: 6 g
- Fiber: 2 g
- Sodium: 294 mg
- Protein: 20 g

Easy Going Avocado And Beef Dish

Prep Time: 5-10 minutes

Cooking Time: 18 minutes

Number of Servings: 4

Ingredients:

- 1 cup cilantro leaves
- 2 ripe avocados, diced
- 2 cups salsa Verde
- 2 beef flank steak, diced
- ½ teaspoon salt
- ½ teaspoon pepper
- 2 medium tomatoes, seeded and diced

Method:

1. Rub beef steak with salt and pepper, season well
2. Pre-heat Ninja Foodi by pressing the "GRILL" option and setting it to "MED" and timer to 18 minutes
3. Let it pre-heat until you hear a beep
4. Arrange diced steak over grill grate, lock lid and cook for 9 minutes
5. Flip and cook for 9 minutes more
6. Take a blender and blend in salsa, cilantro
7. Serve with grilled steak, with blended salsa, tomato, and avocado
8. Enjoy!

Nutritional Values (Per Serving)

- Calories: 520
- Fat: 31 g
- Saturated Fat: 9 g
- Carbohydrates: 38 g
- Fiber: 2 g
- Sodium: 301 mg
- Protein: 41 g

Chapter 6: Snacks

Cajuned Eggplant Appetizer

Prep Time: 5-10 min.

Cooking Time: 10 min.

Number of Servings: 4

Ingredients:

2 tablespoons lime juice

3 teaspoons Cajun seasoning

2 small eggplants, cut into slices (1/2 inch)

1/4 cup olive oil

Directions:

1. Coat the eggplant slices with the oil, lemon juice, and Cajun seasoning.
2. Take Ninja Foodi Grill, arrange it over your kitchen platform, and open the top lid.
3. Arrange the grill grate and close the top lid.
4. Press "GRILL" and select the "MED" grill function. Adjust the timer to 10 minutes and then press "START/STOP." Ninja Foodi will start pre-heating.
5. Ninja Foodi is preheated and ready to cook when it starts to beep. After you hear a beep, open the top lid.
6. Arrange the eggplant slices over the grill grate.
7. Close the top lid and cook for 5 minutes. Now open the top lid, flip the eggplant slices.
8. Close the top lid and cook for 5 more minutes.
9. Divide into serving plates.
10. Serve warm.

Nutritional Values (Per Serving):

Calories: 362
Fat: 11g
Saturated Fat: 3g
Trans Fat: 0g
Carbohydrates: 16g
Fiber: 1g
Sodium: 694mg
Protein: 8g

Honeyed Asparagus

Prep Time: 5-10 min.

Cooking Time: 15 min.

Number of Servings: 4

Ingredients:

2 pound asparagus, trimmed

1/2 teaspoon pepper

1 teaspoon salt

1/4 cup honey

2 tablespoons olive oil

4 tablespoons tarragon, minced

Directions:

1. Combine the asparagus with oil, salt, pepper, honey, and tarragon. Toss well.
2. Take Ninja Foodi Grill, arrange it over your kitchen platform, and open the top lid.
3. Arrange the grill grate and close the top lid.
4. Press "GRILL" and select the "MED" grill function. Adjust the timer to 8 minutes and then press "START/STOP." Ninja Foodi will start pre-heating.
5. Ninja Foodi is preheated and ready to cook when it starts to beep. After you hear a beep, open the top lid.
6. Arrange the asparagus over the grill grate.
7. Close the top lid and cook for 4 minutes. Now open the top lid, flip the asparagus.
8. Close the top lid and cook for 4 more minutes.
9. Serve warm.

Nutritional Values (Per Serving):

Calories: 241
Fat: 15g
Saturated Fat: 3g
Trans Fat: 0g
Carbohydrates: 31g
Fiber: 1g
Sodium: 103mg
Protein: 7.5g

Grilled Maple Broccoli

Prep Time: 5-10 min.

Cooking Time: 10 min.

Number of Servings: 4

Ingredients:

2 heads broccoli, cut into florets

4 tablespoons soy sauce

2 tablespoons canola oil

4 tablespoons balsamic vinegar

2 teaspoons maple syrup

Red pepper flakes and sesame seeds to garnish

Directions:

10. In a mixing bowl, add the soy sauce, balsamic vinegar, oil, and maple syrup. Whisk well and add the broccoli; toss well.
11. Take Ninja Foodi Grill, arrange it over your kitchen platform, and open the top lid.
12. Arrange the grill grate and close the top lid.
13. Press "GRILL" and select the "MAX" grill function. Adjust the timer to 10 minutes and then press "START/STOP." Ninja Foodi will start pre-heating.
14. Ninja Foodi is preheated and ready to cook when it starts to beep. After you hear a beep, open the top lid.
15. Arrange the broccoli over the grill grate.
16. Close the top lid and allow to cook until the timer reads zero.
17. Divide into serving plates.
18. Serve warm with red pepper flakes and sesame seeds on top.

Nutritional Values (Per Serving):

Calories: 141
Fat: 7g
Saturated Fat: 1g
Trans Fat: 0g
Carbohydrates: 14g
Fiber: 4g
Sodium: 853mg
Protein: 4.5g

Potato Chips

Prep Time: 5-10 min.

Cooking Time: 8-10 hours

Number of Servings: 2-3

Ingredients:

1 sweet potato, peeled and cut into slices

½ teaspoon sea salt

½ tablespoon avocado oil

Directions:

9. In a mixing bowl, toss the slice, and oil until evenly coated. Season with the salt to taste.
10. Take Ninja Foodi Grill, arrange it over your kitchen platform, and open the top lid.
11. Arrange the Crisping Basket inside the pot.
12. Press "DEHYDRATE" and adjust the temperature to 120°F. Adjust the timer to 8 hours and then press "START/STOP." Ninja Foodi will start pre-heating.
13. Ninja Foodi is preheated and ready to cook when it starts to beep. After you hear a beep, open the top lid.
14. Arrange the slices in a single layer directly inside the basket.
15. Close the top lid and allow it to cook until the timer reads zero. Dehydrate for 2 more hours if the slices are not crisp enough.
16. Serve warm.

Nutritional Values (Per Serving):

Calories: 146
Fat: 5g
Saturated Fat: 1g
Trans Fat: 0g
Carbohydrates: 22.5g
Fiber: 2g
Sodium: 651mg
Protein: 2g

Grilled Cheese Pineapple

Prep Time: 5-10 min.

Cooking Time: 8 min.

Number of Servings: 4

Ingredients:

Pineapple:

1 pineapple

3 tablespoons honey

2 tablespoons lime juice

1/4 cup packed brown sugar

Dip:

3 ounces cream cheese, softened

1 tablespoon brown sugar

1 tablespoon lime juice

2 tablespoons honey

1/4 cup yogurt

1 teaspoon grated lime zest

Directions:

1. Make 8 wedges from the pineapple and divide each wedge into 2 spears.
2. In a mixing bowl, combine the spears with the sugar, lime juice, and honey; refrigerate for 1 hour.
3. Combine all the dip ingredients in another bowl and set aside.
4. Remove the pineapple spears from the bowl.
5. Take Ninja Foodi Grill, arrange it over your kitchen platform, and open the top lid.
6. Arrange the grill grate and close the top lid.
7. Press "GRILL" and select the "MED" grill function. Adjust the timer to 8 minutes and then press "START/STOP." Ninja Foodi will start pre-heating.
8. Ninja Foodi is preheated and ready to cook when it starts to beep. After you hear a beep, open the top lid.
9. Arrange the spears over the grill grate.
10. Close the top lid and cook for 4 minutes. Now open the top lid, flip the spears.
11. Close the top lid and cook for 4 more minutes.

12. Divide into serving plates.
13. Serve warm with the prepared dip.

Nutritional Values (Per Serving):

Calories: 328
Fat: 6g
Saturated Fat: 1.5g
Trans Fat: 0g
Carbohydrates: 48.5g
Fiber: 8g
Sodium: 98mg
Protein: 7g

Homely Honey Flavored Asparagus

Prep Time: 5-10 minutes

Cooking Time: 15 minutes

Number of Servings: 4

Ingredients:

- 2 pounds asparagus, trimmed
- ½ teaspoon pepper
- 1 teaspoon salt
- ¼ cup honey
- 2 tablespoons olive oil
- 4 tablespoons tarragon, minced

Method:

1. Take a bowl and add asparagus, oil, salt, honey, pepper, tarragon and toss well
2. Pre-heat Ninja Foodi by pressing the "GRILL" option and setting it to "MED" and timer to 8 minutes
3. Let it pre-heat until you hear a beep
4. Arrange asparagus over grill grate, lock lid and cook for 4 minutes, flip asparagus and cook for 4 minutes more
5. Serve and enjoy!

<u>Nutritional Values (Per Serving)</u>

- Calories: 240
- Fat: 15 g
- Saturated Fat: 3 g
- Carbohydrates: 31 g
- Fiber: 1 g
- Sodium: 103 mg
- Protein: 7 g

Subtle Italian Squash

Prep Time: 5-10 minutes

Cooking Time: 16 minutes

Number of Servings: 4

Ingredients:

- 1 medium butternut squash, peeled, seeded and cut into ½ inch slices
- 1 teaspoon dried thyme
- ½ teaspoon salt
- 1 tablespoon olive oil
- 1 and ½ teaspoons dried oregano
- ¼ teaspoon black pepper

Method:

1. Take a mixing bowl and add slices alongside other ingredients, mix well
2. Pre-heat Ninja Foodi by pressing the "GRILL" option and setting it to "MED" and timer to 16 minutes
3. let it pre-heat until you hear a beep
4. Arrange squash slices over the grill grate
5. Cook for 8 minutes, flip and cook for 8 minutes more
6. Serve and enjoy!

Nutritional Values (Per Serving)

- Calories: 238
- Fat: 12 g
- Saturated Fat: 2 g
- Carbohydrates: 36 g
- Fiber: 3 g
- Sodium: 128 mg
- Protein: 15 g

Chapter 7: Dessert

Ranch Flavored Cauliflower Steak

Prep Time: 10 minutes

Cooking Time: 15 minutes

Number of Servings: 4

Ingredients:

- 1 head cauliflower, stemmed and leaves removed
- ¼ cup canola oil
- ½ teaspoon garlic powder
- ½ teaspoon paprika
- Salt and pepper to taste
- 1 cup cheddar cheese, shredded
- Ranch dressing, garnish
- 4 slices bacon, cooked and crumbled
- 2 tablespoons chopped fresh chives

Method:

1. Cut cauliflower from top to bottom into 2-inch steaks, reserve the remaining cauliflower to cook
2. Take a small-sized bowl and whisk in oil, garlic powder, paprika, season with salt and pepper
3. Brush each steak with oil mixture on both sides
4. Pre-heat Ninja Foodi by pressing the "GRILL" option and setting it to "MAX" and timer to 15 minutes
5. let it pre-heat until you hear a beep
6. Transfer steaks to Grill Grate, lock lid and grill for 10 minutes
7. After 10 minutes, flip steaks and top with ½ cup cheese
8. Lock lid and cook for 5 minutes more
9. Once done, drizzle with ranch dressing, top with bacon and chives
10. Enjoy!

Nutritional Values (Per Serving)

- Calories: 720
- Fat: 19 g
- Saturated Fat: 19 g
- Carbohydrates: 11 g

- Fiber: 4 g
- Sodium: 1555 mg
- Protein: 32 g

Choco Pecan Fudge

Prep Time: 5-10 min.

Cooking Time: 35 min.

Number of Servings: 10-12

Ingredients:

½ cup cocoa powder

4 eggs, beaten

2 cups white sugar

½ cup all-purpose flour

2 teaspoons vanilla extract

1 cup pecans, chopped

1 cup butter, melted

Directions:

1. In a mixing bowl, sift together the sugar, flour, and cocoa. Add the eggs, butter, vanilla, and pecans. Combine everything well.
2. Take a multi-purpose pan and lightly grease it with some cooking oil. In the pan, add the prepared batter.
3. Take Ninja Foodi Grill, arrange it over your kitchen platform, and open the top lid.
4. Press "BAKE" and adjust the temperature to 350°F. Adjust the timer to 35 minutes and then press "START/STOP." Ninja Foodi will start pre-heating.
5. Ninja Foodi is preheated and ready to cook when it starts to beep. After you hear a beep, open the top lid.
6. Arrange the pan directly inside the pot.
7. Close the top lid and allow to cook until the timer reads zero.
8. Serve warm.

Nutritional Values (Per Serving):

Calories: 361
Fat: 23.5g
Saturated Fat: 10g
Trans Fat: 0g
Carbohydrates: 39g
Fiber: 3g

Sodium: 91mg
Protein: 4g

Made in the USA
Coppell, TX
25 July 2020